D0404679

The Believer's Secret of Obedience

The Believer's Secret of Obedience

Andrew Murray

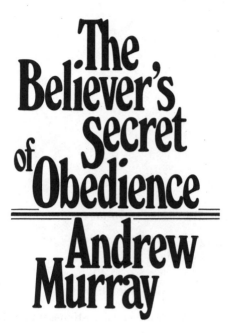

BETHANY HOUSE PUBLISHERS

MINNEAPOLIS, MINNESOTA 55438

A Division of Bethany Fellowship, Inc.

Originally titled *The School of Obedience.*

Copyright © 1982
Bethany House Publishers
All rights reserved

Published by Bethany House Publishers
A Division of Bethany Fellowship, Inc.
6820 Auto Club Road, Minneapolis, Minnesota 55438

Printed in the United States of America

Library of Congress Cataloging in Publication Data

Murray, Andrew, 1828-1917.
 The believer's secret of obedience.

 (The Andrew Murray Christian maturity library)
 Rev. ed. of: The school of obedience. 1935.
 1. Obedience—Religious aspects—Christianity.
I. Title. II. Series.
BV4647.02M87   1982   241'.4   82-14603
ISBN 0-87123-279-0

The Author

ANDREW MURRAY was born in South Africa in 1828. After receiving his education in Scotland and Holland, he returned to that land and spent many years there as both pastor and missionary. He was a staunch advocate of biblical Christianity. He is best known for his many devotional books.

Other Books By Andrew Murray

Contents

CHAPTER ONE

Obedience: Its Place in Holy Scripture

In the study of a Bible word, or of a truth of the Christian life, it helps to examine the place it takes in Scripture. As we see where, how often, and in what connection it is found, its relative importance may be understood as well as its relevance to the whole of revelation. To prepare the way for the study of what obedience is, let me show you where to go in God's Word to find the mind of God concerning it.

First, take scripture as a whole. We begin with Paradise. In Gen. 2:16, we read: "And *the Lord God commanded the man,* saying." And later (3:11), "Hast thou eaten of the tree, whereof *I commanded thee* that thou shouldest not eat?" Note how obedience to the command is the one virtue of Paradise, the one condition of man's abiding there, the one thing his Creator asks of him. Nothing is said of faith or humility or love: obedience includes all. Just as supreme as the claim and authority of God, is the demand for obedience—the one thing that is to decide man's destiny. To obey is the one thing required of man.

Turn now from the beginning to the close of the Bible. In

its last chapter you read (Rev. 22:14), "Blessed are they that *do his commandments,* that they may have right to the tree of life." Or, in the Revised Version, we have the same thought as we read about the seed of the woman (12:17), "that *keep the commandments of God,* and hold the testimony of Jesus"; and of the patience of the saints (14:12), "they that *keep the commandments of God,* and the faith of Jesus." From beginning to end, from Paradise lost to Paradise regained, the law is unchangeable—it is only obedience that gives access to the tree of life and the favor of God.

How was the change effected? From disobedience at the beginning that closed the way to the tree of life, to obedience at the end that again gained entrance to it, turn to that which stands midway between the beginning and the end—the cross of Christ. Read Rom. 5:19, "By *the obedience of one* shall many be made righteous"; or Phil. 2:8, "He . . . *became obedient* unto death, *wherefore* God also hath highly exalted Him"; or Heb. 5:8, 9, "Yet learned he obedience . . . and . . . became the author of eternal salvation unto all them that obey him." In these verses you see how the whole redemption of Christ consists in restoring obedience to its place. The beauty of His salvation consists of this, that He brings us back to the life of obedience, through *which alone the creature can give the Creator the glory due to Him, or receive the glory of which his Creator desires him to partake.* Paradise, Calvary, Heaven, all proclaim with one voice: Child of God, the first and the last thing your God asks of you is simple, universal, unchanging obedience.

Let us turn to the Old Testament. Especially notice how, with any new beginning in the history of God's kingdom, obedience always came into special prominence. Take Noah, the new father of the human race, and you will find four times written (Gen. 6:22; 7:5, 9, 16), "According to all *that God commanded Noah,* so did he." It is the man who does what God commands to whom God can entrust His work, whom God can use to be a savior of men.

Think of Abraham, the father of the chosen race. "By faith Abraham . . . *obeyed*" (Heb. 11:8). When he had been forty years in this school of faith-obedience, God came to perfect his faith, and to crown it with His fullest blessing. Nothing could fit Abraham for this but a crowning act of obedience. When he had bound his son on the altar, God came and said, "By myself have I sworn . . . in blessing I will bless thee, and in multiplying I will multiply thy seed . . . *and in thy seed shall all the nations of the earth be blessed: because thou hast obeyed my voice*" (Gen. 22:16-18).

To Isaac He said, "I will perform the oath which I sware unto Abraham . . . *because that Abraham obeyed my voice*" (Gen. 26:3, 5).

When shall we learn how unspeakably pleasing obedience is in God's sight, and how unspeakable is the reward He bestows upon it? The way to be a blessing to the world is to be men of obedience, known by God and the world by this one mark—a will completely yielded to God's will. Let all who profess to walk in Abraham's footsteps walk thus.

Go on to Moses. At Sinai, God gave him the message to the people, "*If you will obey my voice indeed* . . . ye shall be a peculiar treasure unto me above all people. . ." (Ex. 19:5). In the very nature of things it cannot be otherwise. God's holy will is His glory and perfection; only by obedience to His will is it possible to be His people.

Or take the building of the sanctuary in which God was to dwell. In the last three chapters of Exodus you have the expression nineteen times, "According to all the Lord commanded Moses, so did he." And then: "The glory of the Lord filled the tabernacle."

Again, in Lev. 8 and 9, you have that same expression repeatedly with reference to the consecration of the priests and the tabernacle. And then: "The glory of the Lord appeared unto all the people, and there came a fire out from before the Lord, and consumed . . . the burnt offering. . . ." Words cannot make it plainer, that it is in that which obedience of His people has produced that God delights to dwell, and He crowns the obedient with His favor and presence.

After the forty years' wandering in the wilderness, and its terrible revelation of the fruit of disobedience, there was again a new beginning when the people were about to enter Canaan. Read Deuteronomy and all that Moses spoke when in sight of the land. You will find there is no book of the Bible which uses the word "obey" so frequently or speaks so much of the blessing obedience will assuredly bring. The whole is summed up in the words, "I set before you . . . *a blessing if ye obey* . . . a curse if ye will not obey" (Deut. 11:26-28).

"A blessing if ye obey"—that is the keynote of the blessed life. Canaan, just like Paradise and Heaven, can only be the place of blessing if it is the place of obedience. Would to God we might take it in! Beware of praying only for a blessing. Let us seek for obedience. God will supply the blessing. Let my constant question as a Christian be, "How can I obey and please my God perfectly?"

The next new beginning we have is in the appointment of kings in Israel. In the story of Saul we have the most solemn warning as to the need of exact and entire obedience in a man whom God is to trust as ruler of His people. Saul had been commanded by Samuel to wait seven days for him to come and sacrifice and to show Saul what to do (1 Sam. 10:8). When Samuel delayed (13:8-14) Saul took it upon himself to sacrifice. When Samuel came he said: "Thou hast *not kept the commandment* of the Lord thy God, *which he commanded thee.* . . . Thy kingdom shall not continue . . . because thou hast not kept that which *the Lord commanded thee.*" God will not honor the man who is not obedient.

Saul has a second opportunity given him of showing

what was in his heart. He is sent to execute God's judgment against Amalek. He obeys. He gathers an army of two hundred thousand men, undertakes the journey into the wilderness, and destroys Amalek. But, while God had commanded him to "utterly destroy all that they have, and spare them not," he spared the best of the cattle and Agag. God speaks to Samuel, "It repenteth me that I have set up Saul to be king, for *he . . . hath not performed my commandments.*" When Samuel comes, Saul says, "*I have performed the commandment of the Lord,*" and "*I have obeyed the voice of the Lord.*" And so he had, many would think. But his obedience had not been complete. God claims exact, full obedience. God had said, "Utterly destroy all! Spare not!" This Saul had not done. He had spared the best sheep for a sacrifice unto the Lord. And Samuel said, "*To obey* is better than sacrifice. Because thou hast *rejected the word of the Lord,* he hath rejected thee."

It is a sad type of so much obedience—which in part performs God's commandment, but still is not the full obedience God asks. God says of all sin and all disobedience: "Utterly destroy all! Spare not!" May God reveal to us whether we are indeed doing all He asks, seeking utterly to destroy all and spare nothing that is not in perfect harmony with His will. It is wholehearted obedience, down to the minutest details, that can alone satisfy God. Let nothing less satisfy you. Lest, while we say, "I have obeyed," God says, "You have rejected the word of the Lord."

Just one word more from the Old Testament: Next to Deuteronomy, Jeremiah uses most the word "obey." How sad to see that it is mostly in connection with the complaint that the people had not obeyed. God sums up all His dealings with the fathers in one thought, "I spake not with them concerning sacrifices; but this thing I commanded them, *obey my voice, and I will be your God.*" Would to God that we could learn that all that God speaks of sacrifices, even of the sacrifice of His beloved Son, is subordinate to the one thing—to have man restored to full obedience. Into all the inconceivable meaning of the words, "*I will be your God,*" there is no gateway but this, "*Obey my voice.*"

Now, let us look at the New Testament. Here the prominence our blessed Lord gives to obedience as the one thing for which He was come into the world comes to mind at once. Jesus, who entered it with His, "Lo, I come to do thy will, O God," ever confessed to men, "I seek not my own will, but the will of him that sent me." Of all He did and of all He suffered, even to the death, He said, "This commandment have I received of my Father."

If we turn to His teaching, we find throughout that the obedience He rendered is the same He requires of everyone who would be His disciple. During His whole ministry, from beginning to end, obedience is the very essence of salvation. In the Sermon on the Mount He began with it: No one could enter the kingdom but "he that *doeth the will* of my Father which is in heaven." In the farewell discourse, how wonderfully He reveals the spiritual character of true obedience as it is born of love and inspired by it, and as it also opens the way into the love of God.

"*If ye love me, keep my commandments. And the Father . . . shall give you . . .* the Spirit. . . . *He that hath my commandments, and keepeth them, he it is that loveth me: and he . . . shall be loved of my Father,* and *I will love him, and will manifest myself unto him. If a man love me,* he will *keep my words:* and *my Father will love him,* and *we will come unto him, and make our abode* with him*"* (John 14:15, 16, 21, 23). No words could express more simply or more powerfully the inconceivably glorious place Christ gives to obedience, with its twofold possibility—only possible to a loving heart, but also making possible all that God has to give of His Holy Spirit, His wonderful love, His indwelling through Christ Jesus. I know of no passage in Scripture that gives a higher revelation of the spiritual life, or the power of loving obedience as its one condition. Let us pray God very earnestly that the light of His Holy Spirit may transfigure our daily obedience with heavenly glory.

See how all this is confirmed in the next chapter. How well we know the parable of the vine! How often and how earnestly we have asked the way to abide continually in Christ! We have thought of more study of the Word, more faith, more prayer, more communion with God, but we have overlooked a simple truth. Jesus teaches so clearly, "*If ye keep my commandments, ye shall abide in my love,*" and adds the divine sanction, "*Even as I kept my Father's commandments, and abide in his love.*" For him as for us, the only way under heaven to abide in the divine love is *to keep the commandments.*

Obedience on earth is the key to a place in God's love in heaven. Have you known that? Have you heard it preached? Have you believed it and and proved it true in your experience? Unless there be some likeness between God's wholehearted love in heaven and our wholehearted loving obedience on earth, Christ cannot manifest himself to us, God cannot abide in us, we cannot abide in His love.

If we go on from our Lord Jesus to His apostles, we find in the book of Acts two words of Peter's which show how our Lord's teaching had entered into him. In the one, "God hath given his Holy Spirit *to them that obey him,*" Peter proves how he knew what had been the preparation for Pentecost, the surrender to Christ. In the other, "We *must obey God* rather than man," we have the manward side. Obedience is to be unto death. Nothing on earth dare nor can hinder it in the man who has given himself to God.

Paul uses the expression, "*the obedience to the faith among all nations*" (Rom. 1:5; 16:26), as that for which he was made an apostle. He speaks of what God had done "to make the Gentiles obedient." He teaches that, as the obedience of Christ makes us righteous, we become the *servants of obedience* which leads to righteousness. As disobedience *don't act independently of God.*

in Adam and in us was the one thing that caused death, so obedience, in Christ and in us, is the one thing that the gospel reveals as the way of restoration to God and His favor.

James warns us not to be hearers of the Word only but doers, and explains that Abraham was justified and his faith perfected by his works.

In Peter's first epistle immediately in the first chapter, we see the place obedience has in his system. In verse 2, he speaks to the *"elect . . . through sanctification of the Spirit, unto obedience and sprinkling of the blood of Jesus Christ."* This points to obedience as the eternal purpose of the Father, the great object of the work of the Spirit, and a chief part of the salvation of Christ. In verses 14 and 15 he writes, *"As obedient children"* born of obedience, marked by it, subject to it, ". . . be ye holy in all manner of conversation." Obedience is the starting point of true holiness. In verse 22 we read, "Seeing ye have purified your souls *in obeying the truth. . . ."* The whole acceptance of the truth of God was not merely a matter of intellectual assent or strong emotion; it was a subjection of the life to the dominion of the truth of God. The Christian life was in the first place obedience.

John, we know, uses strong statements. "He that saith, I know him, and *keepeth not his commandments,* is a liar." Obedience is the one hallmark of Christian character. In essence he says, "Let us love *in deed and truth;* hereby we shall assure our hearts before him. . . . And whatsoever we ask, we receive of him, *because we keep his commandments,* and do the things that are pleasing in his sight." Obedience is the secret of a good conscience and of the confidence that God hears us. "This is the love of God, that we *keep his commandments."* The obedience that keeps His commandments is the outward expression by which our hidden, invisible love manifests itself.

Such is the place obedience has in Holy Scripture, in the mind of God, in the hearts of His servants. We may well ask, "Does it take that place in my heart and life?" Have we indeed given obedience that supreme place of authority over us that God means it to have, as the inspiration of every action and of every approach to Him? If we yield ourselves to the searching of God's Spirit, we may find that we never gave obedience the importance it deserves in our scheme of life, and that this is the cause of all our failure in prayer and in work. The deeper blessings of God's grace, and the full enjoyment of God's love and nearness, have been beyond our reach, simply because obedience was never made what God would have it be—the starting point and the goal of our Christian life.

May God arouse in us an earnest desire to know His will fully concerning this truth. Let us pray that the Holy Spirit may show us how far short the Christian's life falls where obedience does not rule all. May He help us see how that life can be exchanged for one of full surrender to absolute obedience, and how sure it is that God in Christ will enable us to live it out. As the disobedience of Adam in Paradise closed its gate, and the obedience of the Second Adam opened it, obedience in us leads us in the new and living way to God's heart, and opens the way for God to come and dwell in our hearts.

May God make obedience—since it is the one sacrifice He asks of us—the one sacrifice we offer Him.

CHAPTER TWO

The Obedience of Christ

"By the obedience of one shall many be made righteous. . . . Know ye not that ye are servants of obedience unto righteousness?" (Rom. 5:19; 6:16).

"By the obedience of one shall many be made righteous." How much we owe to Christ! As in Adam we were made sinners, in Christ we are made righteous. Here we see to what it is in Christ that we owe our righteousness. As Adam's disobedience made us sinners, the obedience of Christ makes us righteous. To the obedience of Christ we owe everything. This is one of the richest among the treasures of our inheritance in Christ. How many have never studied this truth so as to love it and delight in it and get the full blessing of it! May God, by His Holy Spirit, reveal its glory, and make us partakers of its power.

"By the obedience of one shall many be made righteous." Concerning the blessed truth of justification by faith, Paul taught in Rom. 3:21-5:11 what its ever-blessed foundation was—the atonement of the blood of Christ. He showed its way and condition—faith in the free grace of a God who justifies the ungodly. He told of its blessed fruits—the bestowment of the righteousness of Christ, which gives immediate access into the favor of God, and implants the hope of glory.

Then he unfolds the deeper truth of the union with Christ by faith, in which justification has its root, and which makes it possible and right for God to accept us for His sake. Going back to Adam and our union with him, with all the consequences that flowed from that union, Paul proves how perfectly natural and reasonable it is that those who receive Christ by faith, and are so united with Him, become partakers of His righteousness and His life. Paul especially emphasizes the contrast between the disobedience of Adam, with the condemnation and death it caused, and the obedience of Christ, with the righteousness and the life it brings. As we study the place Christ's obedience takes in His work for our salvation, and see in it the very root of our redemption, we shall know what place to give it in our heart and life.

"By one man's disobedience many were made sinners." How was this? There was a twofold connection between Adam and his descendants—*the judicial* and *the vital.* Through the judicial the whole race, though yet unborn, came at once under the sentence of death. "Death reigned from Adam to Moses, even over them"—such as little children—"that had not sinned after the similitude of Adam's transgression." This judicial relation was rooted in the vital connection. The sentence could not have come upon them if they had not been in Adam. Again the vital became the manifestation of the judicial; each child of Adam enters life under the power of sin and death. "By one man's disobedience many were made sinners," both by position subject to the curse of sin and by nature subject to its power.

Adam is the figure of Him who was to come, and who is called the Second Adam, the Second Father of the race. Adam's disobedience in its effects is the exact similitude of what the obedience of Christ becomes to us. When a sinner believes in Christ, he is united to Him, and by a judicial sentence is at once pronounced and accepted as righteous in God's sight. The judicial relationship is rooted in the vital. He has Christ's righteousness only by having Christ himself, and being in Him. Before he knows much of what it means to be in Christ, he can know himself acquitted and accepted. But he is then led on to know the vital connection and to understand that, equally real and complete as was his participation in Adam's disobedience with the death and sinful nature that followed, so is his participation in Christ's obedience, with the righteousness, obedient life and nature that come from it.

The one thing God asked of Adam in Paradise was obedience. The one thing by which a creature can glorify God, or enjoy His favor and blessing, is obedience. The one cause of the power of sin in the world and the ruin it has caused is disobedience. From Adam we have inherited a tendency to willfulness, to selfishness, to disobedience. The whole curse of sin on us is due to Adam's disobedience which we also have chosen. The whole power of sin working in us is nothing but this—that as we inherit Adam's fallen nature, we inherit this tendency to disobedience. By our own choice we become "the children of disobedience." Clearly, the one work Christ was needed for was to remove this disobedience—its curse, its dominion, its evil nature and workings. Disobedience was the root of all sin and misery. The first object of His salvation was to cut away the evil root and restore man to his original destiny—a life in obedience to his God.

How did Christ do this? First, by coming as the Second Adam to undo what the first had done. Sin had made us believe that it humiliated one to be always seeking to know and do God's will. Christ came to show us the nobility, the blessedness, the heavenliness of obedience. When God gave us the robe of creaturehood to wear, we knew not that its beauty, its unspotted purity, came from obedience to God. Christ came and put on that robe that He might show us how to wear it, and how with it we could enter into the presence and glory of God. Christ came to overcome and so bear away our disobedience, and to replace it by His own obedience. As universal, as mighty, as all-prevailing as was the disobedience of Adam, even far more so was to be the power of the obedience of Christ.)

The object of Christ's life of obedience was threefold:

As our *example*, to show us what true obedience was.

As our *surety*, by His obedience to fulfill all righteousness for us.

As our *head*, to prepare a new and obedient nature to impart to us.

So He died, too, to show us that His obedience means a readiness to obey to the uttermost, to die for God. It means the vicarious endurance to the life of God for Him and for us. The disobedience of Adam, wherever it touched, was to be renounced and replaced by the obedience of Christ. Judicially, by that obedience we are made righteous. Just as we were made sinners by Adam's disobedience, we are at once, completely, justified and delivered from the power of sin and death. We stand before God as righteous men. Vitally—for the judicial and the vital are as inseparable as in the case of Adam—we are made one plant with Christ in His death and resurrection, so that we are as truly dead to sin and alive to God as Christ is. And the life we receive in Him is no other than a life of obedience.

To know what obedience is, consider well that the obedience of Christ is the secret of the righteousness and salvation I find in Him. Obedience is the very essence of that righteousness. Obedience is salvation. His obedience, first of all to be accepted, and trusted, and rejoiced in, as covering and swallowing up and making an end of my disobedience, is the one unchanging, never-to-be-forsaken ground of my acceptance. Then, just as Adam's disobedience was the power that ruled my life, and was the power of death in me, Christ's obedience becomes the life-power of the new nature

in me. Then I understand why Paul in this passage so close-
ly links the righteousness and the life. "For if by one man's
offence death reigned by one; much more they which receive abundance of grace, and of the gift of righteousness,
shall reign in life by one, Jesus Christ," ever here on earth.
"The free gift came upon all men unto justification *of life.*"

The more carefully we trace the parallel between the
first and Second Adam, and see how in the former the death
and the disobedience reigned in his seed equally with himself, and how both were equally transmitted through union
with him, the more will the conviction be forced upon us
that the obedience of Christ is equally to be ours, not only
by imputation, but by personal possession. It is so inseparable from Him that to receive Him and His life is to receive
His obedience. When we receive the righteousness which
God offers us so freely, it at once points us to the obedience
out of which it was born, with which it is inseparably one, in
which alone it can live and flourish.

This connection is shown in the next chapter. After having spoken of our life-union to Christ, Paul, for the first
time in the epistle (6:12, 13), gives an injunction, "Let not
sin therefore reign, . . . but yield yourselves unto God," and
then he immediately proceeds to teach how this means
nothing but obedience. "Know ye not . . . his servants ye
are to whom ye obey; whether of sin unto death, or of obedience unto righteousness?" Your relation to obedience is a
practical one; you have been delivered from disobedience
(Adam's and your own), and now are become servants of
obedience, and that "unto righteousness." Christ's obedience resulted in righteousness—the righteousness which is
God's gift to you. Your subjection to obedience is the one
way in which your relation to God and to righteousness can
be maintained. Christ's obedience leading to righteousness
is the beginning of life for you; your obedience leading to
righteousness is its continuance.

There is but one law for the head and the members. As

surely as it was with Adam and his seed, disobedience and death, it is with Christ and His seed, obedience and life. The one bond of union, the one mark of likeness, between Adam and his seed was disobedience. *The one bond of union between Christ and His seed, the one mark of resemblance,* is obedience. It was obedience that made Christ the object of the Father's love (John 10:17, 18) and our Redeemer. *Obedience alone* can lead us in the way to dwell in that love (John 14:21, 23) and enjoy that redemption.

"By the obedience of One shall many be made righteous." Everything depends upon our knowledge of and participation in obedience as the gateway and the path to the full enjoyment of righteousness. At conversion righteousness is given to faith, once for all, completely and for ever, even though there is little or no knowledge of obedience. But as the righteousness is indeed believed in and submitted to, and its full dominion over us, as "servants of righteousness," sought after, its blessed nature will be revealed to us, as born out of obedience, and therefore ever leading us back to its divine origin. The truer our hold of the righteousness of Christ, in the power of the Spirit, the more intense will be our desire to share in the obedience out of which it sprang. In this light let us study the obedience of Christ that like Him we may live as servants of obedience that will result in righteousness.

In Christ *this obedience is a life principle.* Obedience with Him did not mean a single act of obedience now and then, not even a series of acts, but the spirit of His whole life. "I *came,* not to do my own will." "Lo, I *come,* to do thy will, O God." He had come into the world for one purpose: He only lived to carry out God's will. The one supreme, all-controlling power of His life was obedience. He is willing to make it so in us. This was what He promised when He said, "Whosoever shall *do the will* of my Father which is in heaven, the same is my brother and sister and mother." The link in a family is a common life shared by all and a family likeness. The bond between Christ and us is that He and we together do the will of God.

In Christ this obedience was a joy. "I delight to do thy will, O my God." "My meat is to do the will of him that sent me." Our food is refreshment and vitality. The healthy man eats his bread with gladness. But food is more than enjoyment—it is a necessity of life. Doing the will of God was the food that He hungered after and without which He could not live, the one thing that satisfied His hunger, the one thing that refreshed and strengthened Him and made Him glad. It was something of this David meant when he spoke of God's word being "sweeter than honey and the honeycomb." As this is understood and accepted, obedience will become more natural to us and necessary to us, and more refreshing even than our daily food.

In Christ this obedience led to a waiting on God's will. God did not reveal all His will to Christ at once, but day by day, according to the circumstance of the hour. In His life of obedience there was growth and progress; the most difficult lesson came last. Each act of obedience fitted Him for the new discovery of the Father's further command. He said, "Mine ears hast thou opened. . . . I delight to do thy will, O God." As obedience becomes the passion of our life, our ears will be opened by God's Spirit to wait for His teaching, and we will be content with nothing less than divine guidance into the divine will for us.

In Christ this obedience led to death. When He spoke, "I came . . . not to do my own will, but the will of him that sent me," He was ready to go to any length in denying His own will and doing the Father's. He meant it. In nothing My will; at any cost God's will. This is the obedience to which He calls us and for which He empowers us. This wholehearted surrender to obedience in everything is the only true obedience, the only power that is able to carry us through. Would to God that Christians could understand that nothing less than this is what God rightly claims.

Nothing less than this will bring the soul gladness and strength. As long as there is a doubt about obedience, and with that a lurking feeling of possible failure, we lose the confidence that insures victory.

But once we see that God asks total obedience—and promises help for it—we dare offer nothing less. We yield ourselves for His divine power to work, for His Holy Spirit to master our whole life.

In Christ this obedience sprang from the deepest humility. The Authorized Version says, "Have this mind in you, which was also in Christ Jesus, who . . . *emptied himself*" —who *took the form of a servant,* who *humbled himself,* "becoming obedient even unto death." It is the man who is willing for entire self-emptying, is willing to be and live as a servant, "a servant of obedience," is willing to be humbled very low before God and man, to whom the obedience of Jesus will unfold its heavenly beauty and its power. There may be a strong will that secretly trusts in self, that strives for obedience, and fails. As we sink low before God in humility, meekness, patience, and entire resignation to His will, and are willing to bow in an absolute helplessness and dependence on Him, as we turn away wholly from self, it will be revealed to us that the one duty and blessing of a creature is to obey this glorious God.

In Christ this obedience was of faith—in entire dependence upon God's strength. "I can do nothing of myself." "The Father that dwelleth in me doeth the works." The Son's unreserved surrender to the Father's will was met by the Father's unceasing and unreserved gift of His power working in the Son. Even so it will be with us. If we learn that our yielding our will to God is the measure of the power He gives us, we shall see that a surrender to full obedience is nothing but complete faith that God will work all in us. God's promises of the New Covenant rest on this. "The Lord thy God will circumcise thine heart to love the Lord thy God *with all thine heart,* and *thou shalt obey* the Lord thy God." "I will put my Spirit within you, and *cause* you to walk in my statutes, and *ye shall keep* my judgments." Let us, like the Son, believe that God works all in us, and we shall have the courage to yield ourselves to an unreserved obedience—an obedience unto death. That surrender to God will lead to our conformity to God's Son, who did His Father's will because He counted on His Father's power. Let us give our all to God. He will work His all in us.

Do you know that, being made righteous by Christ's obedience, you are like Him and in Him are servants of obedience which leads to righteousness? In the obedience of the One the obedience of the many has its root, life and security. Turn and gaze upon, study and believe in Christ, as the obedient One, as never before. Let this be the Christ we receive and love and seek to be made conformable to. As His righteousness is our one hope, let His obedience be our one desire. Let the sincerity of our faith in God's power at work in us be proven by our accepting the obedient Christ as our very life, the Christ who dwells in us.

CHAPTER THREE

The Secret Of True Obedience

"... Yet learned he obedience ..." (Heb. 5:8).

The secret of true obedience, I believe, is a clear and close personal relationship to God. All our attempts to achieve full obedience will fail until we get access to His abiding fellowship. *It is God's holy presence, consciously abiding with us, that keeps us from disobeying Him.* Defective obedience is always the result of a defective life. To rouse and spur on that defective life by arguments and motives may help, but only to make us feel the need of a different life, a life so entirely under the power of God that obedience will be its natural outcome. The defective life, the life of broken and spasmodic fellowship with God, must be healed, and make way for a full and healthy life; then full obedience will become possible. The secret of true obedience is *the return to close and continual fellowship with God.*

We read that Christ "learned obedience." Why was this necessary? The Word proceeds to explain that He "learned ... obedience by the things which he suffered, and ... became the author of eternal salvation to all them that obey him." Suffering is unnatural to us, and therefore calls for

33

the surrender of our will. Christ needed suffering to learn to obey through it and give up His will to the Father at any cost. He needed to learn obedience so that as our great High Priest He might be made perfect. He learned obedience. He became obedient unto death that He might become the author of our salvation. He became the author of salvation *through obedience* that He might save those *"who obey him."* As obedience was with Him absolutely necessary to procure salvation, so with us it is absolutely necessary to inherit it. The very essence of salvation is obedience to God. Christ as the obedient One saves us as His obedient ones. Whether in His suffering on earth or in His glory in heaven, whether in himself or in us, obedience is what the heart of Christ is set upon.

On earth Christ was a learner in the school of obedience; in heaven He teaches it to His disciples here on earth. In a world where disobedience reigns and results in death, the restoration of obedience is in Christ's hands. In His own life and in ours He has undertaken to maintain it. He teaches and works it in us. Think about what—and how—He teaches. How much have we yielded ourselves to be pupils in His school where obedience is to be learned? When we think of an ordinary school, the principal elements are the teacher, the textbooks, the pupils. What are each of these in Christ's school of obedience?

The Teacher

"He learned obedience." And now that He teaches it, He does so first and mainly by unfolding the secret of His own obedience to the Father. I said that the power of true obedience is to be found in a clear personal relationship to God. It was so with our Lord Jesus. Of all His teaching He said, "I have not spoken of myself, but the Father which sent me gave me a commandment, what I should say and what I should speak. And I know that his commandment is life everlasting; whatever I speak therefore, even as the Father said unto me, so I speak." This does not mean that in eternity Christ received God's commandment as part of the Father's commission to Him upon entering the world. No. Day by day, each moment as He taught and worked, He lived, as man, in continual communication with the Father and He received the Father's instructions just when needed. Does He not say, "The Son can do nothing of himself but what he *seeth* the Father do; for the Father *showeth* the Son all things that himself *doeth*; and he *will show* him greater things." "As *I hear,* I judge." "I am not alone, but I and the Father that sent me." "The words that I speak, I speak not of myself, but the Father that dwelleth in me"? Everywhere He reveals dependence upon a present fellowship and operation of God, a hearing and a seeing of what God speaks and does and shows.

Our Lord ever spoke of His relation to the Father as the type and the promise of our relation to Him, and to the Father through Him. With us as with Him, *the life of continual obedience is impossible without continual fellowship and continual teaching.* Only when God comes into our lives in a degree and a power which many never consider possible, when His presence as the Eternal and Ever-present One is believed and received even as the Son believed and received it, can there be any hope of a life in which every thought is brought into captivity to the obedience of Christ.

2 Cor. 10:5

The imperative need to receive our orders and instructions continually from God himself is implied in the words "Obey my voice, and I will be your God." The expression "obeying the commandments" is seldom used in Scripture; it is almost always, obeying *Me,* or obeying or hearkening to *My voice.*

With an army commander, a schoolteacher, or the father of a family, it is not the code of laws and its rewards or threats—clear and good—that secures true obedience. It is the personal living influence, awakening love and enthusiasm. With us it is the joy of ever hearing the Father's voice that will give the joy and the strength of true obedience. It is the voice that gives power to obey the word; the word without the living voice does not avail.

How clearly Israel illustrates this. The people had heard the voice of God on Sinai, and were afraid. They asked Moses that God not speak to them anymore. They wanted Moses to receive the Word of God and bring it to them. They only thought of the commands. They knew not that *the only power to obey* is in the presence of God and His voice speaking to us. And so with only Moses and the tables of stone to speak to them, their whole history is one of disobedience, because they were afraid of direct contact with God. It is the same today. Many, many Christians find it so much easier to take their teaching from godly men than to wait upon God and receive it from Him. Their faith stands in the wisdom of men and not in the power of God.

Our Lord, "who learned obedience" by every moment waiting to see and hear the Father, has a great lesson to teach us. *It is only when, like Him, with Him, in and through Him, we continually walk with God, and hear His voice,* that we can possibly attempt to offer God the obedience He asks and promises to work in us.

Out of the depths of His own life and experience, Christ can give and teach us this. Pray earnestly that God may show you the folly of attempting to obey without the same strength that even Christ needed. Pray to be willing to give up everything for the Christlike joy of the Father's presence all the day.

The Textbook

Christ's direct communication with the Father did not take away His need of Holy Scripture.

In the divine school of obedience there is only one

textbook, whether for the elder brother or the younger children. In learning obedience He used the same textbook as we have. Not only when He had to teach or to convince others did He appeal to the Word. He needed it and He used it for His own spiritual life and guidance. From the beginning of His public life to its close He lived by the Word of God. "*It is written*" was the sword of the Spirit with which He conquered Satan. "The Spirit of the Lord God is upon me"; this word of scripture was the consciousness with which He opened His preaching of the Gospel. "That the scripture might be fulfilled" was the light in which He accepted all suffering, and even gave himself to the death. After the resurrection He expounded to the disciples "in all the scriptures the things *concerning himself*." In Scripture He had found God's plan and path for Him marked out. He gave himself to fulfill it. In the use of God's Word He received the Father's continual direct teaching.

In God's school of obedience the Bible is the only textbook. By this we know the disposition in which we are to come to the Bible—with the simple desire to find there God's will concerning us and to do it. Scripture was not written to increase our knowledge but to guide our conduct —"that the man of God may be perfect, thoroughly furnished *unto all good works.*" "If any man will *do,* he shall know." Learn from Christ to consider all there is in Scripture of the revelation of God. His love and His counsel, as simply auxiliary to God's great end: that the man of God may be fitted to do His will as it is done in heaven, and that man may be restored to that perfect obedience of which God's heart is set, where alone lies blessedness.

To apply the Word in Christ's own life and conduct, to know when each particular portion was to be believed and carried out, Christ needed and received divine teaching. It is He who speaks in Isaiah, "The Lord God wakeneth morning by morning, he wakeneth mine ear to hear as the learned; the Lord God hath opened mine ear." Even so does

He who thus learned obedience teach us, by giving us the Holy Spirit in our heart, as the Divine Interpreter of the Word. This is the great work of the indwelling Holy Spirit, to draw the Word we read and think upon *into our heart,* and make it quick and powerful there, so that God's living Word may work effectively in our will, our love, our whole being. It is because this is not understood that the Word has no power to work obedience.

Let me be very plain about this. We rejoice in increased attention given to Bible study, and in testimonies about the interest awakened and benefit received. But let us not deceive ourselves. We may delight in studying the Bible, we may admire and be charmed with the views we get of God's truth; the thoughts suggested may make a deep impression and waken the most pleasing religious emotions, and yet the practical influence in making us holy or humble, loving, patient, ready either for service or suffering, may be very small. The one reason for this is that we do not receive the Word as it truly is—the Word of a living God, who must himself speak it to us and into us if it is to exert its divine power. However we study and delight in the letter of the Word, it has no saving or sanctifying power. Human wisdom and human will, however strenuous their effort, cannot give or command that power. The Holy Spirit is the mighty power of God. *It is only as the Holy Spirit teaches you,* only as the gospel is preached to you by man or by book, "with the Holy Ghost sent down from heaven," that you will be given, along with every command, the strength to obey and work in you the very thing commanded.

With man, knowing and willing, knowing and doing, even willing and performing, are often separate for lack of power, and sometimes even at variance. But, *never in the Holy Spirit.* He is at once the light and might of God. All He is and does and gives contains equally the truth and the power of God. When He shows you God's command, He always shows it to you as a possible and a certain thing, a divine life and gift prepared for you, which He who shows is able to impart.

It is only when Christ, through the Holy Spirit, teaches you to understand and take the Word into your heart that He can really teach you to obey as He did. Every time you open your Bible, believe that just as surely as you listen to the divine, Spirit-breathed Word, so surely will our Father, in answer to the prayer of faith and docile waiting, give the Holy Spirit's living operation in your heart. Let all your Bible study be a thing of faith. Do not only believe the truths or promises you read. This may be in your own power. But *believe in the Holy Spirit; in His being in you; in God's working in you through Him*. Receive the Word into your heart, in the quiet faith that He will enable you to love it, yield to it, and keep it. Then our blessed Lord Jesus will make the book to you what it was to Him when He spoke of "the things which are written concerning me." All Scripture will become the simple revelation of what God is going to do for you, in you, and through you.

The Pupil

We have seen how our Lord teaches us obedience by unfolding the secret of His learning it, in unceasing dependence on *the Father*. We have seen how He teaches us to use the Sacred Book, as He used it, as a divine revelation of what God has ordained for us, with *the Holy Spirit* to expound and enforce it. If we now consider the place the believer takes in the school of obedience as pupil, we shall better understand what *Christ the Son* requires to do an effective work in us.

In a faithful student several things make up his feelings toward a trusted teacher: complete submission and perfect trust while giving just as much time and attention as his teacher asks. When we see and consent that Jesus Christ has a right to all this, we may hope to experience how wonderfully He can teach us an obedience like His own.

The true pupil, say of some great musician or painter, yields his master *a wholehearted and unhesitating submission*. In practicing the scales or mixing colors, in the slow and patient study of the elements of his art, the student knows that it is wisdom simply and fully to obey. It is this wholehearted surrender to His guidance, this implicit submission to His authority, Christ asks. We come to Him asking Him to teach us the lost art of obeying God as He did. He asks us if we are ready to pay the price. It is entirely and utterly to deny self! It is to give up our will and our life to the death! It is to be ready to do whatever He says! The only way of learning to do a thing is to do it. The only way of learning obedience from Christ is to give up your will to Him, and to make the doing of His will the one desire and delight of your heart. Unless you take the vow of absolute obedience as you enter this class in Christ's school, it will be impossible for you to make any progress.

The true scholar of a great master finds it easy to render him this implicit obedience, simply because the pupil *trusts* his teacher. The student gladly sacrifices his own wisdom and will, to be guided by a higher. We need this confidence in our Lord Jesus. He came from heaven to learn obedience that He might be able to teach it well. His obedience is the treasury out of which, not only the debt of our past disobedience is paid, but also grace for our present obedience is supplied. In His divine power over our hearts and lives, He invites, He deserves, He wins our trust. By the power of a personal admiration and attachment to himself, by the power of His divine love, shed into our heart by the Holy Spirit and awakening within us a responsive love, Jesus awakens our confidence and communicates to us the true secret of success in His school. Just as fully as we have trusted Him as a Savior to atone for our disobedience, now let us trust Him as a teacher to lead us out of it. Christ is our Prophet or Teacher. A heart that enthusiastically believes in His power and success as a teacher will, in the joy of that faith, find it possible and easy to obey. It is the presence of Christ with us all the day that will be the secret of true obedience.

A scholar gives his master just as much of *his attendance and attention* as is asked. The master determines how much time must be devoted to personal interchange and instruction. Obedience to God is such a heavenly art, our nature is so utterly foreign to it, the path in which the Son himself learned it was so slow and long, that we must not wonder if it does not come at once. *Nor must we wonder if it needs more time at the Master's feet in meditation, prayer and waiting, in dependence and self-sacrifice, than most are ready to give.* But let us give it. In Christ Jesus heavenly obedience has become human again; obedience has become our birthright and our life-breath. Let us cling to Him, let us believe and claim His abiding presence. With Jesus Christ, who learned obedience as our Savior and who teaches obedience as our Master, we can live lives of obedience. We cannot emphasize too much that His obedience is our salvation; in Him, the living Christ, we find it and partake of it moment by moment. Let us beseech God to show us how Christ and His obedience are actually to be our life every moment; that will then make us pupils who give Him all our heart and all our time. And He will teach us to keep His commandments and abide in His love, *even as He* kept His Father's commandments and abides in His love.

CHAPTER FOUR

The Morning Watch in the Life of Obedience

"For if the firstfruit be holy, the lump is also holy; and
if the root be holy, so are the branches" (Rom. 11:16).

How wonderful and blessed is the divine appointment of
the first day of the week as a holy day of rest. Not just to
have one day of rest and spiritual refreshment amid the
weariness of life, but so that one holy day, at the beginning
of the week, might sanctify the whole, might help and fit us
to carry God's holy presence into all the week and its work.
With the firstfruit holy, the whole lump is holy; with the
root holy, all the branches are holy too.

How gracious, too, is the provision suggested by so many
types and examples of the Old Testament, by which a
morning hour at the beginning of the day enables us to obtain a blessing for all its work, and gives us the assurance of
power for victory over every temptation. How unspeakably
gracious that in the morning hour the bond that unites us
with God can be so firmly tied that during hours when we
have to move amid the rush of men or duties, and can
scarcely think of God, the soul can be kept safe and pure.

How good that the soul can so give itself away in the time of secret worship into His keeping that temptation shall only help to unite it closer to Him. What cause for praise and joy, that the morning watch can each day so renew and strengthen the surrender to Jesus and the faith in Him that the life of obedience can not only be maintained in fresh vigor, but can indeed go on from strength to strength.

In this chapter I want to consider the "morning watch" in connection with the subject of obedience. How intimate and vital that connection is. The desire for a life of total obedience will give new meaning and value to the morning watch, just as it can alone give the strength and courage needed for this obedience.

Think first of the *motive principle* that will make us love and faithfully keep the morning watch. If we do it simply as a duty and a necessary part of our religious life, it will very soon become a burden. Or, if the main thought be our own happiness and safety, that will not supply the power to make it truly attractive. Only one thing will suffice to keep us faithful—*the desire for fellowship with God.* For that we were created in God's likeness; in that we hope to spend eternity. It alone can fit us for a true and blessed life, either here or hereafter. To have more of God, to know Him better, to receive from Him the communication of His love and strength, to have our life filled with His—for this He invites us to enter the inner chamber and shut the door.

It is in the closet, in the morning watch, that our spiritual life is both tested and strengthened. *There* is the battlefield where it is decided every day whether God is to have all, whether our life is to be absolute obedience. If we truly conquer there, committing ourselves into the hands of our Almighty Lord, the victory during the day is sure. It is *there,* in the inner chamber, proof is to be found whether we really delight in God, and make it our aim to love Him with our whole heart.

Let our first lesson be this: the presence of God is the

most important thing in our devotions. To meet God, to yield ourselves to His holy will, to know that we please Him, to have Him give us our orders, and lay His hand upon us, and bless us, and say to us, "Go in this thy strength"—it is when the soul learns that this is what is to be found in the morning watch, day by day, that we shall learn to long for it and delight in it.

The reading of God's Word is part of what occupies us there. With regard to this I have more than one thing I wish to emphasize.

One is that unless we beware, the Word which is meant to point us the way to God, may actually intervene and hide Him from us. The mind may be occupied and interested and delighted at what it finds, but still, because this is more head knowledge than anything else, it may do us little good. If it does not lead us to wait on God, to glorify Him, to receive His grace and power for sweetening and sanctifying our lives, it becomes a hindrance instead of a help.

Another lesson that cannot be repeated too often, or pressed too urgently, is, that it is only by the teaching of the Holy Spirit that we can get at the real meaning of what God means by His Word. Only by the Spirit will the Word really reach into our inner life and work in us. The Father in heaven, who gave us His Word from heaven, with its divine mysteries and message, has given us His Holy Spirit within, to explain and internally appropriate that Word. The Father wants us to ask each time that He teach us by His Spirit. He wants us to bow in a meek, teachable frame of mind, and believe that the Spirit will, in the hidden depth of our heart, make His Word live and work. He wants us to remember that the Spirit is given to us that we should be led by Him, should follow Him, should have our whole life under His rule, and that, therefore, He cannot teach us in the morning unless we honestly give up ourselves to His leading. But if we do this, and patiently wait on Him, not to get new thoughts, but to get the power of the Word in our heart, we can count upon His teaching. Let your closet be the classroom, let your morning watch be the study hour, *in which your relation of entire dependence on, and submission to, the Holy Spirit's teaching is proved to God.*

Thirdly, in confirmation of what was said above: always study God's Word in the spirit of an unreserved surrender to obey. You know how often Christ and His apostles in their epistles speak of hearing and not doing. If you accustom yourself to study the Bible without an earnest and very definite purpose to obey, you're getting hardened in disobedience. Never read God's word concerning you without honestly yielding yourself to obey it at once and asking grace to do so. God has given us His Word to tell us what He wants us to do, and to show the grace He has provided to enable us to do it. How sad to think it a pious thing just to read that Word without any earnest effort to obey it! May God keep us from this terrible sin! Let us make it a sacred habit to say to God, *"Lord, whatever I know to be Your will, I will at once obey."* Always read with a heart yielded up in willing obedience.

Once again, I have here referred to commands we already know, and which are easily understood. But, remember, there are a great many commands to which your attention may never have been directed or others with so wide and unceasing application that you have not grasped it yet. Read God's Word with a deep desire to know all His will. If there are things which appear difficult, commands which look too high, or for which you need divine guidance to tell you how to carry them out—and there are many such—let them drive you to seek divine teaching. It is not the text that is easiest and most encouraging that brings most blessing, but the text, whether easy or difficult, which throws you most upon God. God would have you "filled with the knowledge of his will in all wisdom and spiritual understanding." This wonderful work is to be done in the closet. Remember, it is only when you know that *God is telling you to do a thing* that you feel sure He gives the strength to do it. Only as we are willing to know all God's will, will He reveal more of it to us from time to time. Only then will we be able to do it all.

What a power the morning watch may be in the life of a student who makes a determined resolve to meet God there: to renew the surrender to absolute obedience, humbly and patiently to wait on the Holy Spirit to be taught all God's will, and to receive the assurance that every promise given him in the Word will infallibly be made true. He that prays this way for himself will become a true intercessor for others. In the light of these thoughts I now want to explain *what prayer is to be* in the morning watch.

— First, secure the presence of God. Do not be content with anything less than seeing the face of God, having the assurance that He is looking on you in love, and listening and working in you. If our daily life is to be full of God, how much more the morning hour, where the life of the day alone can have God's seal stamped upon it. In our religion we want nothing so much as *more of God*—His love, His will, His holiness, His Spirit living in us, His power working in us for men. There is no way of getting this except by close personal communion. And there is no time so good for securing and practicing it as the morning watch. The superficiality and feebleness of our religion and religious work all come from having so little real contact with God. If it be true that God alone is the fountain of all love and good and happiness, and that to have as much as possible of His presence and His fellowship, of His will and His service, is our truest and highest happiness, then surely to meet Him alone in the morning watch ought to be our first care. To have had God appear to them, and speak to them, was the secret of the obedience and strength of all the Old Testament saints. Give God time in secret so to reveal himself that your soul may call the name of the place Peniel—"for I have seen him face to face."

Next, let the renewal of your surrender to absolute obedience for that day be a main part of your morning sacrifice. Let any confession of sin be very definite—a plucking out and cutting off of everything that has been grieving to God. Let any prayer for grace for a holy walk be just as definite—an asking and accepting in faith of the very grace and strength you are especially in need of. Let your outlook on the day you are entering on be a very determined resolve that obedience to God shall be its controlling principle. There is no surer way—there is no other possible way—of getting into God's love and blessing in prayer than by getting into His will. In prayer, yield yourself absolutely to the blessed will of God. This will avail more than much asking. Beseech God to show you this great mercy, to allow and enable you to enter into His will and abide there—that will make the knowing and doing His will in your life a blessed certainty. Let your prayer indeed be a "morning sacrifice," placing yourself as a whole burnt offering on the altar of the Lord. The measure of surrender to full obedience will be the measure of confidence toward God.

Remember that true prayer and fellowship with God cannot be all from one side. We need to be still, to wait and hear what response God gives. *This is the office of the Holy Spirit, to be the voice of God to us.* In the hidden depths of the heart, He can give a secret but most certain assurance that we are heard, that we are well-pleasing, that the Father engages to do for us what we have asked. To hear the voice and receive this assurance, we need the quiet stillness that waits on God, the quiet faith that trusts in God, the quiet heart that bows in nothingness and humility before God and allows Him to be all in all. When we wait on God to take His part in our prayer, the confidence will come to us that we will receive what we ask, that our surrender of ourselves in the sacrifice of obedience is accepted, and that therefore we can count upon the Holy Spirit to guide us into all the will of God, just as He means us to know and do it.

What glory would come to us in the morning watch, and through it into our daily life, if it were thus made an hour spent with the Triune God, for the Father, through the Son and the Spirit, to take conscious possession of us for the day. How little need there would be to urge and plead with God's children to keep the morning watch.

And now comes the last and the best of all. In the obedience of our Lord Jesus, just as in all His fellowship with the Father, the essential element was—it was all for others. This Spirit flows through every member of the body. The more we know it and yield to it, the more will our life be what God would make it.

The highest form of prayer is intercession. The chief object for which God chose Abraham and Israel and us was to make us a blessing to the world. We are a royal priesthood—a priestly people. As long as prayer is only a means of personal improvement and happiness, we cannot know its full power. Let intercession be a real longing for the souls of those around us, a real bearing of the burden of their sin and need, a real pleading for the extension of God's kingdom, real labor in prayer for definite purposes to be realized. Let such intercession be what the morning watch is consecrated to, and see what new interest and attraction it will have.

Intercession! Oh, to realize what it means. To take the name, and the righteousness, and the worthiness of Christ, to put them on, and in them to appear before God! "In Christ's stead"—now that He is no longer in the world—to beseech God by name for individual men and their needs, where His grace can do its work! With faith in our own acceptance, and the anointing of the Spirit to fit us for the work, to know that our prayer can avail to "save a soul from death," can bring down and dispense the blessings of heaven upon earth! To think that in the hour of the morning watch this work can be renewed and carried on day by day, each prayer closet maintaining its own separate communication with heaven, and helping together in bringing down its share of the blessing. In intercession, more than in the zeal that works in its own strength with little prayer, the highest type of piety, the true Christlikeness, is cultivated. In intercession a believer rises to his true nobility in the power of imparting life and blessing. It is intercession we must look to for any large increase of the power of God in the Church and its work for men.

In conclusion, turn back and think again about the intimate and vital connection between obedience and the morning watch. Without obedience there cannot be the spiritual power to enter into the knowledge of God's Word and will. Without obedience there cannot be the confidence, the boldness, the liberty that knows that it is heard. Obedience is fellowship with God in His will; without it there is not the capacity for seeing and claiming and holding onto the blessings He has for us. So, on the other side, without definite living communion with God in the morning watch, the life of obedience cannot possibly be maintained. There the vow of obedience can every morning be renewed in power and confirmed from above. There the presence and fellowship can be secured which make obedience possible. It is there that by the obedience of the One, and our union with Him, strength is received for all that God asks. There the spiritual understanding of God's will is received, which leads to a walk worthy of the Lord to all well-pleasing.

God has called us to live a wonderful, heavenly, altogether supernatural life. Let the morning watch each day be to you as the open gate of heaven, through which light and power stream into your waiting heart, and from which you go out to walk with God all the day.

CHAPTER FIVE

The Entrance to the Life of Full Obedience

"Obedient unto death" (Phil. 2:8).

Obedient unto death. I plan to explain in this chapter about the entrance into that life of obedience. You might think it a mistake to take this text, in which you have obedience in its very highest perfection, as our subject in considering the entrance on the course. But it is no mistake. The secret of success in a race is to have the goal clearly defined and aimed at from the very outset. *"He became obedient unto death."* There is no other Christ for any of us, no other obedience that pleases God, no other example for us to copy, no other teacher from whom to learn to obey. Christians suffer inconceivably because they do not from the outset heartily accept this as the only obedience at which they are to aim. From the beginning the youngest Christian will find it a strength in the school of Christ to make nothing less than this his prayer and his vow: *obedient unto death*. It is at once the beauty and the glory of Christ; to share in it is the highest blessing He has to give; the desire for and the surrender to it is possible to the youngest believer.

A story in ancient history illustrates this obedience. A proud king, with a great army following him, demands submission from the king of a small but brave nation. When the ambassadors have delivered their message, the king calls on one of his soldiers to stab himself. At once he does it. A second is called; he too obeys at once. A third is summoned; he too is obedient to death. "Go and tell your master that I have three thousand such men. Let him come." The king dared count upon men who didn't hold their life dear to them when the king's word called for it. God wants such obedience. Such obedience is what Christ gave. It is such obedience He teaches—let it be that same obedience and nothing less we seek to learn. From the very outset of the Christian life let us aim to avoid the fatal mistake of calling Christ Master, but not doing what He says. Let all who are in any degree convicted of the sin of disobedience come and listen. God's Word will show us the way to escape from disobedience and gain access to the life Christ can give—a life of full obedience.

1. Confession and Cleansing of Disobedience

Obviously this must be the first step. In Jeremiah (the prophet who more than any other speaks of the disobedience of God's people), God says, "Return, thou backsliding Israel, saith the Lord; for I am merciful. *Only acknowledge thine iniquity, that ye have not obeyed my voice,* saith the Lord God. Turn, O backsliding children, saith the Lord." Just as there hardly can be pardon at conversion without confession, neither can there be, after conversion, deliverance from the overcoming power of sin, and the disobedience it brings, without a new and deeper conviction and confession. Our disobedience must not be confessed in a vague generality; the specific things in which we actually disobey must be definitely uncovered, confessed, abandoned, and given into Christ's hands, and by Him cleansed away. Only then can there be hope of entering into the way of true obedience. Let us search our life in the light of our Lord's teaching.

Christ appeals to the law. He came not to destroy the law but to ensure its fulfillment. To the young ruler He said, "Thou knowest the commandments." Let the law be our first test. Let us take a single sin—such as lying. I once had a note from a young lady saying that she wished to obey fully and that she felt compelled to confess an untruth she had told me. It was not a matter of importance, and yet, she rightly judged that the confession would help her to be cleansed. How much there is in society that will not stand the test of strict truthfulness.

There are other commandments, also, up to the very last, which condemn all coveting and lusting after what is not ours, and in which too frequently the Christian yields to disobedience. All this must completely end; we must confess our disobedience, and in God's strength put it away forever, if there is to be any thought of our entering a life of full obedience.

Christ revealed the new law of love. To be as merciful as the Father in heaven, to forgive just as He does, to love our enemies and do good to them that hate us, and live lives of self-sacrifice and beneficence—this was the religion Jesus taught on earth. Let us consider an unforgiving spirit when we are provoked or ill-used, unloving thoughts and sharp or unkind words, the neglect of the call to show mercy and do good and bless, as disobedience which must be felt and mourned over and plucked out like a right eye, before the power of a full obedience can be ours.

Christ spoke much of self-denial. Self is the root of all lack of love and obedience. Our Lord called His disciple to deny himself and to take up his cross; to forsake all, to hate and lose his own life; to humble himself and become the servant of all. He did so, because self—self-will, self-pleasing, self-seeking—is simply the source of all sin. When we indulge the flesh in such a simple thing as eating and drinking; when we gratify self by seeking or accepting or rejoicing in what indulges our pride; when self-will is allowed to assert itself, and we make provision for the fulfillment of its desire, we are guilty of disobedience to His command. This gradually clouds the soul and makes the full enjoyment of His light and peace an impossibility.

Christ claimed for God the love of the whole heart. For himself He equally claimed the sacrifice of all to come and follow Him. The Christian who has not in his heart definitely made this his aim, who has not determined to seek for grace so to live, is guilty of disobedience. Much in his religion may appear good and earnest, but he cannot possibly have the joyful consciousness of knowing that he is doing the will of his Lord and keeping His commandments.

When the call is heard to come and now begin anew a true life of obedience, there are many who desire to do so, and try quietly to slip into it. They think that by more prayer and Bible study they will grow into it—it will gradually come. They are greatly mistaken. The word God uses in Jeremiah might teach them their mistake. "Turn, O backsliding children," turn to Me. A soul that is in full earnest and has taken the vow of full obedience may grow out of a feeble obedience into a fuller one. But there is no growing out of disobedience into obedience. A turning back, a turning away, a decision, a crisis, is needed. And that comes only by the very definite insight into what has been wrong, and the confession of that with shame and penitence. Then alone will the soul seek for that divine and mighty cleansing from all its filthiness which prepares for the consciousness of the gift of the new heart, and God's Spirit in it, causing us to walk in His statutes. If you would hope to lead different lives, to become possessors of a Christlike obedience unto death, begin by beseeching God for the Holy Spirit of conviction, to show you all your disobedience and to lead you in humble confession to the cleansing God has provided. Rest not till you have received it.

2. Faith That Obedience Is Possible

This is the second step. To take that step we must try to understand clearly what obedience is.

To this end we must observe carefully the difference between voluntary and involuntary sin. It is with the former alone that obedience deals. We know that the new heart which God gives His child is placed in the midst of the flesh with its sinful tendency. Out of this there often arise, even in one who is walking in true obedience, evil suggestions of pride, unlovingness, impurity, over which he has no direct control. They are in their nature utterly sinful and vile; but they are not imputed to a man as acts of transgression. They are not acts of disobedience, which he can break off and cast out, as he can the disobedience of which we have spoken. The deliverance from them comes in another way, not through the will of the regenerate man, by which obedience always comes, but through the cleansing power of the blood and the indwelling Christ. As the sinful nature rises, all he can do is to abhor it and trust in the blood that at once cleanses him and keeps him clean.

It is extremely important to note the distinction. It keeps the Christian from thinking obedience impossible. It encourages him to seek and offer his obedience in the sphere where it can be effective. In direct proportion to which the power of the will for obedience is utilized continually, so can the power of the Spirit be obtained and trusted to do the cleansing work in what is beyond the reach of the will.

When this difficulty has been removed, there is often a second one that arises, to make us doubt whether obedience be indeed possible. Men connect it with the idea of absolute perfection. They put together all the commands of the Bible; they think of all the graces these commands point to, in their highest possible measure; and they think of a man with all those graces, every moment in their full perfection, as an obedient man. How different is the demand of the Father in heaven! He takes into account the different powers and attainments of each child of His. He asks of him only the obedience of each day, or rather, each hour at a time. He sees whether I have indeed chosen and given myself up to the wholehearted performance of every known command. He sees whether I am really longing and learning to know and do all His will. And when His child does this, in simple faith and love, the obedience is acceptable. The Spirit gives us the sweet assurance that we are well-pleasing to Him, and enables us to "have confidence before God, because we know that we keep his commandments, and do the things that are pleasing in his sight." This obedience is indeed an attainable degree of grace. The faith that it is truly attainable is indispensable to the obedient walk.

You ask for the ground of that faith in God's word? You find it in God's New Covenant promise, "I will write my law in their heart. I will put my fear in their heart, and they shall not depart from me." The great defect of the Old Covenant was that it demanded but did not provide the power for obedience. This the New Covenant did. The heart means the love, the life. The law put into, written into the heart, means that it has taken possession of the inmost life and love of the renewed man. The new heart delights in the law of God; it is willing and able to obey it. Do you doubt this? Does your experience not confirm it? No wonder. A promise of God is a thing of faith. You do not believe it and so cannot put it in use.

To illustrate, you know what invisible ink is. You write on paper with it, but nothing can be seen by one watching. Tell him the secret and although he still cannot see, he accepts it by faith. Hold it up to the sun, or put a chemical on it, and the secret writing appears. Just so is God's law written in your heart. If you believe this firmly, and come and say to God that His law is there in your inmost part, and hold up that heart to the light and heat of the Holy Spirit, you will find it true. The law written in the heart will mean to you the fervent love of God's commands *with the power to obey them.*

A story is told of one of Napoleon's soldiers. The doctor was seeking to extract a bullet that had lodged in the region of the heart, when the soldier cried, "Cut deeper; you will find Napoleon graven there." Christian, do you believe that the law lives in your inmost being? Speak in faith the words of David and of Christ, "I delight to do thy will, O God! Yea, thy law *is written* on my heart." The faith of this will assure you that obedience is possible; such faith will help you into the life of true obedience.

3. The Step from Disobedience to Obedience Through Surrender to Christ

"Turn to me, ye backsliding children, and I will heal your backsliding," God said to Israel. They were His people, but had turned from Him; the return must be immediate and complete. To turn our back upon the divided life of disobedience, and in the faith of God's grace to say, "I will obey," may be the work of a moment.

The power for it, to take the vow and to maintain it, comes from the living Christ. We have said before, the power of obedience lies in the mighty influence of a living personal Presence. As long as we take our knowledge of God's will from a book or from men, we will only fail. If we take Jesus, in His unchanging nearness, as both our Lord and our Strength, we can obey. The voice that commands is the voice that inspires. The eye that guides is the eye that encourages. Christ becomes all in all to us: the Master who commands, the Example who teaches, the Helper who strengthens. Turn from your life of disobedience to Christ. Give yourself to Him in surrender and faith.

In surrender) Let Him have all. Give up your life to be as full of Him, of His presence, His will, His service, as He can make it. Give yourself to Him, not only to be saved from disobedience, or just to be happy, but to live your own life without sinning and trouble. Yield so completely that He may have you wholly for himself, as a vessel, as a channel, which He can fill with himself, with His life and love for men, and use in His blessed service.

In faith.) When a soul sees this new strength in Christ, the power for continual obedience, it needs a new faith to comprehend the special blessing of His great redemption. The former faith only understood of His atonement, "He became obedient unto death," its motive to love and obedience. The new faith learns to take the word as Scripture speaks it, "*Have this mind in you,* which was also in Christ Jesus, who humbled himself, becoming obedient even unto death." It believes that Christ has put His own mind and Spirit into us, and in the faith of that, prepares to live and act it out.

God sent Christ into the world to restore obedience to its place in our heart and life, to restore man to His place in the obedience to God. Christ came, and, becoming obedient unto death, proved what the only true obedience is. He lived it out, and perfected it in himself, as the life that He won through death, and now communicates to us. The Christ who loves us, who leads and teaches and strengthens us, who lives in us, is the Christ who was obedient unto death. "Obedient unto death" is the very essence of the life He imparts. Shall we not accept it and trust Him to manifest it in us?

Would you enter into the blessed life of obedience? See here the open gate—Christ says, "I am the door." See here the new and living way—Christ says, "I am the way." We begin to see it: all our disobedience was because of our not knowing Christ aright. We see it: obedience is only possible in a life of unceasing fellowship with himself. The inspiration of His voice, the light of His eyes, the grasp of His hand make it possible, make it certain.

Come and let us bow down, and yield ourselves to this Christ. Obedient unto death, in the faith that He makes us partakers with himself of all that He is and all that He has.

CHAPTER SIX

The Obedience of Faith

"By faith Abraham . . . obeyed" (Heb. 11:8).

"By faith Abraham, when he was called to go out into a place, which he should after receive for an inheritance, obeyed; and he went out, not knowing whither he went." He believed that there was a land of Canaan of which God had spoken. He believed in it as a "land of promise," guaranteed to him as an inheritance. He believed that God would bring him there, would show it to him, and give it to him. In that faith he dared to go out, not knowing whither he went. In the blessed ignorance of faith he trusted God, and obeyed, and received the inheritance.

The land of promise that has been set before us is the blessed life of obedience. We have heard God's call to us to go out and dwell there—about that there can be no mistake. We have heard the promise of Christ to bring us there and to give us possession of the land—that too is clear and sure. Do we desire that all our life and work be lifted up to the level of a holy and joyful obedience, and that through us God make obedience the keynote of our Christian life? If so, our aim is high. We can reach it only by a new inflow of the power that comes from above. Only by a faith that gets a new vision and lays hold of the powers of the heavenly world, which are secured to us in Christ, can we obey and obtain the promise.

Let us review the different themes we have been considering.

There is the "Morning Watch." We purpose that our observance of it shall be faithful and spiritual. We are looking to God to daily make it such direct fellowship with Him, such surrender to Him and His will, as shall lift the whole person into His presence and service for the whole day.

There is Bible study. We have seen that doing God's will is the only key to the knowledge of God's truth. We have been challenged to read the Bible without the slightest hesitation about our giving immediate obedience to every command.

There is the spiritual help we are to give those around us, in watching over each other in tender humility and love, and seeking the edification of others as much as our own.

There is aggressive work: laboring for the unsaved, not only at special seasons, but at all times, in the patient perseverance of prayer and love. This is not easy. It is only possible when the sense of duty is inspired by the joy of His presence, who commands us to do the work.

Then there is the work in wider sphere—evangelistic and missionary.

As we think of all this, of cultivating in ourselves and others the conviction that we live only to please Him, and to serve His purposes, some are ready to say, "This is not a land of promise we are called to enter, but a life of burden and difficulty and certain failure." Do not say so. God calls you indeed to a land of promise. Come and prove what He can work in you. Come and experience the nobility of a Christlike obedience unto death. Come and see what blessing God will give to him who, with Christ, gives himself to the uttermost unto the ever-blessed and most holy will of God. Only believe in the glory of this good land of wholehearted obedience: in God, who calls you to it; in Christ, who will bring you in; in the Holy Spirit, who dwells in you and enables you to obey. He that believes enters in.

In thinking of our consecration, I wish to speak of the obedience of faith, and of faith as the sufficient power for all obedience. Five simple declarations are expressive of the disposition of a believing heart, who enters into that life in the good land: I see it, I desire it, I expect it, I accept it, I trust Christ for it.

1. Faith Sees It

In the foregoing chapters I tried to show you the map of the land, and to indicate the most important places in that land—the points at which God meets and blesses the soul. What we need now, by faith, quietly and definitely is to settle the question: Is there really such a land of promise, in which continuous obedience is certainly, is divinely possible? As long as there is any doubt on this point, it is out of the question to go up and possess the land.

Just think of Abraham's faith. It rested in God, in His omnipotence and His faithfulness. I have put before you the promises of God. Hear another of them: "I will give you a new heart, and *I will put my Spirit within you,* and *I will cause* you to walk in my judgments, and *ye shall keep* them." Here is God's covenant engagement. He adds, "I the Lord have spoken, and *I will do it.*" He undertakes to cause and enable you to obey. In Christ and the Holy Spirit He has made the most wonderful provision for fulfilling His engagement.

Just do what Abraham did—fix your heart upon God. "He was strong in faith, giving glory to God, being fully persuaded that what he had promised he was able to perform." God's omnipotence was Abraham's stay. Let it be yours. Look at all the promises God's Word gives of a clean heart, a heart established blameless in holiness, of a life in

righteousness and holiness, of a walk in all the commandments of the Lord unblamable and well-pleasing to Him, of
God's working in us to will and to do, of His working in us
that which is well-pleasing in His sight. In simple faith de-
clare: God says this; His power can do it. Let this assurance
possess you: *a life of full obedience is possible.* Faith can see
the invisible and the impossible. Gaze on the vision until
your heart says, "It must be true; it is true; there is a life
promised that until now I have never known."

2. Faith Desires It

When I read the Gospel story and see how ready the sick
and the blind and the needy were to believe Christ's Word, I
often ask myself what it was that made them so much more
ready to believe than we are. The answer I get in the Word
is this, that one great difference lies in the honesty and in-
tensity of the desire. They did indeed desire deliverance
with their whole heart. There was no need of pleading with
them to make them willing to take His blessing.

Alas, that it should be so different with us! All indeed
wish, in a halfhearted way, to be better than they are. But
how few there are who really "hunger and thirst after righteousness"; how few who intensely long and cry for a life of
close obedience and the continual consciousness of being
pleasing to God. There can be no strong faith without
strong desire. Desire is the great motive-power in the uni-
verse. It was God's desire to save us that moved Him to
send His Son. It is desire that moves men to study and work
and suffer. It is desire for salvation alone that brings a sinner to Christ. It is the desire for God, and the closest possible fellowship with Him, the desire to be just what He
would have us to be, and to have as much of His will as possible, that will make the promised land attractive to us. It is
this will that makes us forsake everything to get our full
share in the obedience of Christ.

How can the desire be awakened? How sad that we need to ask the question and that the most desirable of all things—likeness to God in the union with His will and doing it—has so little attraction for us! Let us take it as a sign of our blindness and dullness, and beseech God to give us by His Spirit "enlightened eyes of the heart." Ask that we may see and know "the riches of the glory of our inheritance" waiting upon the life of true obedience. Let us turn and gaze on this life in this light of God's Spirit as truly attainable. Gaze again on it as certain, as divinely secured and divinely blessed, until our faith begins to burn with desire, and to say, "I do long to have it—with my whole heart will I seek it."

3. Faith Expects It

The difference between desire and expectation is great. There is often a strong desire after salvation in a soul who has little hope of really obtaining it. It is a great step in advance when desire passes into expectation, and the soul begins to say of spiritual blessing, "I am sure it is for me, and, though I do not see how, I confidently expect to obtain it." The life of obedience is no longer an unattainable ideal held out by God, to make us strive to get at least a little nearer it, but is become a reality, meant for the life in flesh and blood here on earth. Expect it, as most certainly meant for you; expect God to make it true.

There is much indeed to hinder this expectation. Your past failure; your unfavorable temperament or circumstances; your feeble faith; your apprehension as to what such a devotion, obedient unto death, may demand; your conscious lack of power for it—all this makes you say, "It may be for others; I am afraid it is not for me." I beg you not to talk like this. You are leaving God out of your reasoning. Look up to His power and His love, and begin to say, "This is for me," Then expect to get it.

Take courage from the lives of God's saints who have gone before you. Saint Teresa writes that, after her conversion, she "spent more than eighteen years of my life in that miserable attempt to reconcile God and my life of sin." But at last she was able to write, "I have made a vow never to offend God in the very least matter. I have vowed that I would rather die a thousand deaths than do anything of that kind, knowing I was doing it—this was obedience unto death. I am resolved never to leave anything whatever undone that I consider still to be more perfect, and more for the honor of my Lord."[1]

Gerhard Tersteegen had from his youth sought and served the Lord. After a time the sense of God's grace was withdrawn from him, and for five long years he was as one far away on the great sea, where neither sun nor stars appear. "But my hope was in Jesus." All at once a light broke on him that never went out, and he wrote, with blood drawn from his veins, that letter to the Lord Jesus in which he said, "From this evening to all eternity, Thy will, not mine, be done. Command and rule and reign in me. I yield up myself without reserve, and I promise, with Thy help and power, rather to give up the last drop of my blood than knowingly or willingly be untrue or disobedient to Thee." That was his obedience unto death.

Set your heart upon this, and expect it. The same God lives still. Set your hope on Him: He will do it.

4. Faith Accepts It

To accept is more than to expect. Many wait and hope and never possess because they do not accept. To all who

---

[1]She says further: "We are so long and so slow in giving up our hearts to Thee. And then Thou wilt not permit our possession of Thee without our paying well for so precious a possession. There is nothing in all the world wherewith to buy the shedding abroad of Thy love in our hearts, but *our heart's love.* God never withholds himself from them who pay this price and persevere in seeking Him. He will, little by little, and now and then, strengthen and restore that soul, until it is at last victorious."

have not accepted, and feel as if they are not ready to accept, we say, Expect. If the expectation be from the heart, and be set indeed upon God himself, it will lead the soul to accept. To all who say they do expect, we urgently say, Accept. Faith has the wondrous God-given power to say, "I accept, I take, I have."

It is because of the lack of this definite faith to claim and appropriate the spiritual blessing we desire that so many prayers appear to be fruitless. For such an act of faith all are not ready. In many cases there is not yet the spiritual capacity to accept the blessing, where there is no true conviction of the sin of disobedience, and, alas, no true sorrow for it. Often there is no strong longing or purpose to obey God totally in everything. In others there is no deep interest in the message of Holy Scripture, that God wants to "perfect us to do His will," by himself "working in us that which is pleasing in His sight." In such cases the Christian is content to be a babe. He wants only to suck the milk of consolation. He is not able to bear the strong meat of which Jesus ate, "doing the will of His Father."

And yet we come to all with the entreaty, "Accept the grace for this wonder-filled new life of obedience. Accept it now." Without this your act of consecration will come to little. Without this your purpose to try to be more obedient must fail. Has not God shown you that there is an entirely new position for you to take—an attainable position of simple childlike obedience, day by day, to every command His voice speaks to you through the Spirit; a possible position of simple childlike dependence on an experience of His all-sufficient grace, day by day, for every command He gives? I pray you to take that position, make that surrender, take that grace—now. Accept and enter into the true life of faith, and the unceasing obedience of faith. As unlimited and as sure as God's promise and power are, may your faith be. As unlimited as your faith is, will your simple childlike obedience be. Ask God for His aid, and accept all He has offered you.

5. *Faith Trusts Christ for All*

"All the promises of God are in Christ Jesus, and in him, Amen, unto the glory of God by us." It is possible that as we have considered the life of obedience, there have been questions and difficulties rising to which you cannot at once give an answer. Do you feel as if you cannot take it all in at once? Can you reconcile it with all the old habits of thought and speech and action? Do you fear you will not be able immediately to subject all to this supreme all-controlling principle, "Do everything as the will of God: do all as obedience to Him"? To all these questions there is one answer, one deliverance from all these fears: Jesus Christ, the living Savior, who knows all, and asks you to trust yourself to Him for the wisdom and the power to walk always in the obedience of faith.

We have seen more than once how His whole redemption, as He effected it, is nothing but obedience. As He communicates it, it is still the same. He gives us the spirit of obedience as the spirit of our life. This spirit comes to us each moment through Him. He himself takes charge of our obedience. There is none under heaven except what He has and gives and works. He offers himself to us as surety for the maintenance of our obedience, and asks us to trust Him for it. In Jesus himself all our fears are removed, all our needs supplied, all our desires met. He the righteous One is your righteousness, He the obedient One is your obedience. Will you not trust Him for this? What faith sees and desires and expects and accepts, surely it will dare trust Christ to give and to work.

Will you not today take the opportunity of giving glory to God and His Son by trusting Jesus now to lead you into the promised land? Look up to your glorified Lord in heaven, and in His strength renew, with new meaning, your vow of allegiance, your vow never to do anything knowingly or willingly that would offend Him. Trust Him for the faith to make the vow, for the heart to keep it, for the strength to carry it out. Trust Him, the loving One, by His living presence, to secure both your faith and obedience. Trust Him, and venture to join in an act of consecration, in the assurance that He undertakes to be its Yea and Amen, to the glory of God by us.

CHAPTER SEVEN

The School of Obedience

"Gather up the fragments that remain, that nothing be lost" (John 6:12).

In our study of obedience, there were some points I had no chance to introduce and others I was unable to explain clearly. Now I wish to speak about these, hoping to help those in Christ's school of obedience.

1. On Learning Obedience

First, let me warn against misunderstanding the expression—learning obedience. We are apt to think that absolute obedience as a principle—obedience unto death—is a thing that can only be gradually learned in Christ's school. This is a great and most hurtful mistake. What we have to learn, and do learn gradually, is the practice of obedience, in new and ever more difficult commands. But as to the principle, Christ wants us from the very entrance into His school to vow complete obedience. A little child of five can be as implicitly obedient as a youth of eighteen. The difference between the two lies not in the principle, but in the nature of the work demanded. Though externally Christ's obedience unto death came at the end of His life, the spirit of His obedience was the same from the beginning. Wholehearted obedience is not the end, but the beginning of our school life. The end is fitness for God's service, when obedience has placed us fully at God's disposal. A heart yielded to God in unreserved obedience is the one condition of progress in Christ's school and of growth in the spiritual knowledge of God's will.

Do get this matter settled at once. Remember God's rule: all in exchange for all. Give Him all; He will give you all. Consecration avails nothing unless it means presenting yourself as a living sacrifice to do nothing but the will of God.

2. Of Learning To Know God's Will

This unreserved surrender to obey is the first condition of entering Christ's school, and this alone fits us to receive instruction about the will of God for us. There is a general will of God for all His children which we can, in some measure, learn from the Bible. But there is a special individual application of these commands—God's will concerning each of us personally—which only the Holy Spirit can teach. And He will teach it only to those who have taken the vow of obedience. This is the reason why there are so many unanswered prayers for God to make known His will. Jesus said, "If any man *wills* to do his will, he shall know of the teaching, whether it be of God." If a man's will is really set on doing God's will—if his heart is surrendered to do it and as a consequence, he does it as far as he knows it—then he shall know what God has further to teach him. This is true of every scholar with the art he studies, of every apprentice with his trade, of every man in business—doing is the one condition of truly knowing. So, in the spiritual realm, obedience—doing God's will as far as we know and vowing to do all as He reveals it—fits us to receive the true knowledge of what God's will is for each of us.

In connection with this, three things are essential. Seek a deep sense of your *great ignorance of God's will,* and of your impotence to know it aright by your own efforts. The consciousness of ignorance lies at the root of true teachableness. "The meek will he guide in the way"—those who humbly confess their need of teaching. Head knowledge only gives human thoughts without power. God by His Spirit gives a living knowledge that enters the heart and works effectually.

Cultivate a strong faith that God *will make you know* wisdom in the hidden part, in the heart. Perhaps you have known so little of this in your Christian life until now that the thought appears strange. Learn that God's working and the place where He gives His life and light is in the heart, deeper than all our thoughts. Any uncertainty about God's will makes joyful obedience impossible. Confidently believe that the Father is willing to make known what He wants you to do. Count upon Him for this. Expect it with certainty.

Because of the darkness and deceitfulness of the flesh and the fleshly mind, ask God very earnestly for *the searching and convincing light of the Holy Spirit.* There may be many things which you think lawful or allowable which your Father wants you to forsake. To consider as settled that these things are the will of God just because you and others think so may bar you from knowing God's will for you in the matter. Without reserve, bring everything to the judgment of the Word, explained and applied by the Holy Spirit. Wait on God to lead you to know that everything you are and do is pleasing in His sight.

3. On Obedience unto Death

There is a deeper and more spiritual aspect of this truth. As a rule, it is something that does not come up in the earlier stages of the Christian life. And yet it is needful that every believer know the privileges that await him as he progressively obeys. There is an experience into which wholehearted obedience will bring the believer, where he will know that, as surely as with his Lord, obedience leads to death.

What does this mean? During our Lord's life, His resistance to sin and the world was perfect and complete. Even so, His final deliverance from their temptation, His victory over their power and His obedience were not complete until He had died to the earthly life and to sin. In that death He surrendered His life in perfect helplessness into the Father's hands, waiting to be raised up by Him. Through death He received the fullness of His new life and glory. Through death alone—the giving up of the life He had—could obedience lead Him into the glory of God.

The believer shares with Christ in this death to sin. In regeneration he is baptized into it by the Holy Spirit. Owing to ignorance and unbelief he may know little experimentally of this complete death to sin. When the Holy Spirit reveals to him what he possesses in Christ, and he appropriates it in faith, the Spirit works in him the very same disposition which animated Christ in His death. With Christ it was a total ceasing from His own life, a helpless committal of His spirit into the Father's hands. He completely fulfilled the Father's command: Lay down Your life in My hands. Out of the perfect self-oblivion of the grave He entered into the glory of the Father.

Into this same fellowship the believer is brought. He finds that even in the most unreserved obedience for which God's Spirit fits him, there still remains a secret element of self and self-will. He longs to be delivered from it. In God's Word he is taught that this can only be by death. The Spirit helps him to claim more fully that He is indeed dead to sin in Christ, and that the power of that death can work mightily in him. He is made willing to be obedient unto death, this total death to self, which makes him truly nothing. In this he finds a full entrance into the life of Christ. To see the need of this complete death to self and to be made willing for it, then to be led into the total self-emptying and humility of our Lord Jesus—this is the highest lesson our obedience has to learn. This is indeed Christlike obedience unto death.

There is no room here to enlarge on this. In due time, God himself will teach this lesson to those who are entirely faithful.

4. Of the Voice of Conscience

In regard to the knowledge of God's will, we must give conscience its place and submit to its authority. In a thousand little things the law of nature or education teaches us what is right and good, but even earnest Christians do not always feel themselves bound to obey these. If you are unfaithful in that which is least, who will entrust you with greater things? Not God. If the voice of conscience tells you of a course of action that is nobler or better, and you choose something else because it is easier or pleasing to self, you unfit yourself for the teaching of the Spirit by disobeying the voice of God. A strong will always to do the right and to do the very best that conscience points out is a will to do God's will. Paul writes, "I lie not, my conscience bearing me witness in the Holy Ghost." The Holy Ghost speaks through conscience. If you disobey and hurt conscience, you make it impossible for God to speak to you. Obedience to God's will is shown by a sensibility and respect for the voice of conscience. This is true with regard to eating and drinking, sleeping and resting, spending money and seeking pleasure. Let everything be brought into subjection to the will of God.

This leads to another thing of great importance. If you would live the life of true obedience, see that you maintain a good conscience before God, and never knowingly indulge in anything which is contrary to His mind. Along with his

love of God's Word, George Muller attributed all his happiness during seventy years to the fact that "he had maintained a good conscience in all things, not going on in a
course he knew to be contrary to the will of God." Conscience is the guardian or monitor God has given you, to
warn when anything goes wrong. To the limits of the light
you have, give heed to conscience. Ask God, by the teaching
of His will, to give more light. Seek the witness of conscience as to whether you are obeying that light. Conscience
will become your encouragement and your helper, and give
you the confidence that your obedience is accepted and
your prayer for ever-increasing knowledge of God's will is
heard.

5. Of Legal and Evangelistic Obedience

Even when the vow of unreserved obedience has been
taken, there may still be two sorts of obedience—that of the
law, and that of the Gospel. Just as there are two Testa-
ments, an Old and New, so there are two styles of religion,
two ways of serving God.

This is what Paul speaks of in Romans when he says,
"Sin shall not have dominion over you: for ye are *not under
the law* but under grace" (6:14), and further speaks of our
being freed—"delivered from the law," so that we "serve in
newness of the spirit, and *not in the oldness of the letter*"
(7:6). Again he reminds us, "For ye have not received the
spirit of bondage again to fear: but ye have received the
spirit of adoption. . ." (8:15). The threefold contrast points
very evidently to a danger existing among those Christians
of still acting as if they were under the law, serving in the
oldness of the letter and in the spirit of bondage. One great
cause of the feebleness of so much Christian living is that it
is more under law than under grace. What is the difference?

What the law demands from us, grace promises and performs for us. The law deals with what we ought to do—
whether we can or not—and by appealing to motives of fear

and love stirs us to do our utmost. But the law gives no real strength, and so only leads to failure and condemnation. Grace points to what we cannot do, but offers to do it for us and in us. The law comes with commands on stone or in a book; grace comes in a living gracious Person, who gives His presence and His power. The law promises life if we obey. Grace gives life, even the Holy Spirit, with the assurance that we can obey.

Human nature is ever prone to slip back out of grace into the law, and secretly to trust in trying and doing its utmost. The promises of grace are so divine, the gift of the Holy Spirit *to do all in us* is so wonderful, that few believe it. This is the reason they never dare take the vow of obedience, or, having taken it, they turn back again. Study well what gospel obedience is. The Gospel is good tidings. Its obedience is part of that good tidings—*that grace, by the Holy Spirit, will do all in you.* Believe that. Obey in the joyful hope that comes from faith—a faith in the exceeding abundance of grace, in the mighty indwelling of the Holy Spirit, in the blessed love of Jesus, whose abiding presence makes obedience not only possible but certain.

6. *Of the Obedience of Love*

This is one of the special and most beautiful aspects of gospel obedience. The grace which promises to work all through the Holy Spirit is the gift of eternal love. The Lord Jesus (who takes charge of our obedience, teaches it, and by His presence secures it to us) is He who loved us unto death, who loves us with a love that passes knowledge. Nothing can receive or know love but a loving heart. This loving heart enables us to obey. Obedience is our loving response to the divine love resting on us, and is our only access to a fuller enjoyment of that love.

How our Lord insisted upon that in His farewell discourse! Three times He repeats it in John 14: "*If ye love me, keep my commandments.*" "He that hath my commandments, and keepeth them, he it is that *loveth me.*" "If a man *love me,* he will keep my words." Is it not clear that love alone can give the obedience Jesus asks, and receive the blessing Jesus gives to obedience? The gift of the Spirit, the Father's love and His own, with the manifestation of himself; the Father's love and His own making their abode with us—all these things are made possible to us by loving obedience.

In the next chapter He shows from the other side how obedience leads to the enjoyment of God's love—He kept His Father's commandments, and *abides in His love.* If we keep His commandments, we shall *abide in His love.* He proved His love by giving His life for us. *We are His friends.* We shall enjoy His love if we do what He commands us. Between His first love and our love in response to it, between our love and His fuller love in response to ours, *obedience is the one indispensable link.* True and full obedience is impossible, except as we live in love. "This is the love of God, that we keep his commandments."

Beware of a legal obedience, striving after a life of true obedience under a sense of duty. Ask God to show you the "newness of life" which is needed for a new and full obedience. Claim the promise, "I will circumcise thine heart, to love the Lord thy God with all thy heart; and thou shalt obey the Lord thy God." Believe in the love of God and the grace of our Lord Jesus. Believe in the Spirit given in you, enabling you to love, and so causing you to walk in God's statutes. In the strength of this faith and in the assurance of sufficient grace, that is made perfect in weakness, enter into God's love and the life of living obedience it works. *Nothing but the continual presence of Jesus in His love can fit you for continual obedience.*

7. Is Obedience Possible?

This question lies at the very root of our life. The secret, half-unconscious thought—that to live always well-pleasing to God is beyond our reach—eats away the very root of our strength. I strongly urge you to give a definite answer to the question.

Do you still fear that obedience is not possible—even in the light of God's provision for obedience, of His promise of working out His good pleasure in you, and of His giving you a new heart, with the indwelling of His Son and Spirit? Then ask God to open your eyes to truly know His will.

If you are convinced in your mind and agree with this truth theoretically but are still afraid to surrender yourself to such a life, ask God to open your eyes and enable you to know *His will for yourself*.

Beware lest the secret fear of having to give up too much, of having to become too exclusive and entirely devoted to God, keep you back.

Beware of seeking just enough religion to ease your conscience, and as a result to lose the desire to do and be and give God all He is worthy of.

Beware, above all, of "limiting" God, of making Him a liar, by refusing to believe what He has said He can and will do. If our study is to be of any profit, do not rest until you have truly learned that daily obedience to all that God wills for you is possible. In His strength yield yourself to Him for it.

But on one condition only. Not in the strength of your resolve or effort. But yield to *the unceasing presence of Christ and the unceasing teaching of the Spirit of all grace and power*. Christ, the obedient One, living in you, will assure your obedience. That obedience will be to you a life of love and joy in His fellowship.

CHAPTER EIGHT

Obedience to the Last Command

"Go ye therefore and teach all nations" (Matt. 28:19).

"Go ye into all the world and preach the gospel to every creature" (Mark 16:15).

"As thou didst send me into the world, even so send I them into the world" (John 17:18; 20:21).

"Ye shall receive power, when the Holy Spirit is come upon you: and ye shall be my witnesses unto the uttermost part of the earth" (Acts 1:8).

These words breathe nothing less than the spirit of world conquest. "All the nations," "all the world," "every creature," "the uttermost part of the earth"—each expression indicates that the heart of Christ was set on claiming His rightful dominion over the world He had redeemed and won for himself. And He counts on His disciples to undertake and carry out the work. As He stands at the foot of the throne, ready to ascend and reign, He tells them, "All authority hath been given unto me in heaven and on earth," and points them at once to "all the world," to "the uttermost part of the earth," as the object of His and their desire and efforts. As the King on the throne, He himself will be their Helper: "I am with you alway." They are to be the advance-guard of His conquering hosts, even unto the end of the world. He himself will carry on the war. He seeks to inspire them with His own assurance of victory, with His own purpose of making this the only thing worth living or dying for—the winning back of all the world to its God.

Christ does not teach or argue, ask or plead; He simply commands. He has trained His disciples to obedience. He has attached them to himself in a love that can obey. He has already breathed His own resurrection Spirit into them. He can count upon them. He dares to say to them: "Go ye into all the world." Before, during His life on earth, they had more than once expressed their doubt about the possibility of fulfilling His commands. But here, as quietly and simply as He speaks these divine words, they accept them. No sooner has He ascended than they go to the appointed place to wait to be equipped by their Lord with heavenly power for heaven's work of making all the nations His disciples. They accepted the command and passed it on to those who through them believed on His name. Within a generation, simple men, whose names we do not even know, had preached the gospel in Antioch and Rome and the regions beyond. The command was passed on and absorbed into the heart and life, as meant for all ages, as meant for every disciple.

The command is for each one of us, too. There exists in the Church of Christ no privileged clan to which alone belongs the honor, nor any servile clan on which alone rests the duty, of carrying the Gospel to every creature. The life Christ imparts is His own life. The Spirit He breathes is His very own Spirit. The one disposition He works is His own self-sacrificing love. By the very nature of His salvation every member of His body, in full and healthy access with Him, feels urged to impart what he has received. The command is no arbitrary law from without; it is simply the revelation which awaits our intelligent and voluntary consent, of the full and wonderful truth. We are His body. We now occupy His place on earth. His will and love now carry out through us the work He began, and now in His stead we live to seek the Father's glory in winning a lost world back to Him.

How terribly the Church has failed in obeying the command! How many Christians there are who don't know that such a command exists! How many hear of it but do not wholeheartedly try to obey it! How many seek to obey it— but only in the way and to the degree as seems fitting and convenient to them! We have professed to yield ourselves to wholehearted obedience. Surely we are prepared to listen gladly to anything that can help us to understand and carry out our Lord's last and great command: *the Gospel to every creature*. What I have to say falls under three simple headings: *Accept His command. Place yourself entirely at His disposal. Begin at once to live His kingdom.*

1. Accept His Command

Various things weaken the force of this command. There are the impressions that a command general in its nature, and given to all, is not as binding as one that is entirely personal and specific; that if others do not their part, our share of the blame is comparatively small; that where the difficulties are very great, obedience cannot be absolutely demanded; and that if we are willing to do our best, this is all that can be asked of us. These attitudes are not obedience. This is not the spirit in which the first disciples obeyed. This is not the spirit in which we wish to live with our beloved Lord. Why not resolve that, even if no one else does, I, by His grace, will give myself and my life to live for His kingdom. Let me for a moment forget all others and think of my personal relation to Jesus.

I am a member of Christ's body. He expects every member to be at His disposal, to be animated by His Spirit, to live for what He is and does. It is so with my body. I carry every healthy member with me day by day in the assurance that I can count upon it to do its part. Our Lord has so truly made me a part of His body that He can ask and expect this same cooperation from me. And I have so truly yielded myself to Him that there can be no idea of my wanting anything except to know and to do His will.

Take the illustration of the "Vine and the Branches." The branch, like the vine, has only one object for its being—bearing fruit. If I really am a branch, I am—just as much as He was in the world—only and wholly to bring forth fruit, to live and labor for the salvation of men.

Take still another illustration. Christ has bought me with His blood. No slave conquered by force or purchased by money was ever so entirely the property of his master as my soul, redeemed and won by Christ's blood, given up and bound to Him by love. My soul is His property, for Him alone to do with it what He pleases. He claims it by divine right, working through the Holy Spirit in infinite power, and I have given full assent to live wholly for His kingdom and service. This is my joy and my glory.

There was a time when it was different. There are two ways in which a man can bestow his money or service on another. Once long ago there was a slave, who by his trade earned much money. All the money came to the master. The master was kind and treated the slave well. At length, from earnings his master had allowed the slave, he was able to purchase his liberty. In course of time the master became impoverished, and had to come to his former slave for help. He was not only able, but most willing to give it, and gave liberally, in gratitude for former kindness.

You see at once the difference between the bringing of his money and service when he was a slave, and his gifts when he was free. In the former case he gave all, because both he and his money belonged to the master. In the latter he only gave what he chose. In which way ought we to give to Christ Jesus? I fear many, many give as if they were free to give whatever they choose, whatever they think they can afford. The believer, to whom the right which the purchase price of the blood has acquired has been revealed by the Holy Spirit, delights to know that he is the bond slave of redeeming love, and to lay everything he has at his Master's feet, because he belongs to Him.

Have you ever wondered that the disciples accepted the great command so easily and so heartily? They came fresh from Calvary, where they had seen the blood. They had met the risen One and He had breathed His Spirit into them. During the forty days, "through the Holy Ghost" He had given His commandments to them. To them Jesus was Savior, Master, Friend and Lord. His word had divine power; they could only obey. Let us bow at His feet and yield to the Holy Spirit to reveal and assert His mighty claim. Let us unhesitatingly and with the whole heart accept the command and our one life purpose: the Gospel to every creature!

2. Place Yourself at His Disposal

The last great command has been so strongly linked with foreign missions that many are inclined to confine it to them exclusively. This is a great mistake. Our Lord's words, "Make disciples of all nations; teaching them to observe all things whatsoever I commanded you," tell us our aim. It is to be nothing less than to make every man a true disciple, living in holy obedience to all Christ's will. And what a work there is to be done in our Christian churches and our so-called Christian communities before it can be said that the command has been carried out! How much the whole Church and every believer in it need to realize that this work is the sole object of its existence! To bring the Gospel in a full, persevering, saving way to every creature is the mission and ought to be the passion of every redeemed soul. This alone is the Spirit and likeness and life of Christ formed in you.

If the Church needs to preach one thing, in the power of the Holy Ghost, it is the absolute and immediate duty of every child of God, not only to take such part in this work as he may think fit or possible, but to give himself to Christ the Master, to be guided and used as He would have. And therefore I say to every reader who has taken the vow of full obedience—and dare we count ourselves true Christians if we have not done so?—place yourself at once and wholly at Christ's disposal. As binding as is the first great command on all God's people, "Thou shalt love the Lord thy God, with all thy heart," is this last great command too—"The Gospel to every creature." Before you know what your work may be, before you feel any special desire or call or fitness for any work—if you are willing to accept the command, place yourself at His disposal. As Master He will train and fit and guide and use you. Fear not; come now and forever out of the selfish religion which puts your own will and comfort first and gives Christ only what you see fit. Let the Master know that He can have you wholly. Volunteer at once for His service.

These simple words, "It is my purpose, if God permit, to become a foreign missionary," have brought countless blessings into thousands of lives! It helped them surrender in obedience to the great command, and became a milestone in their history. Many who never can go abroad, or who think so because they have not asked their Master's will, might be blessed if they would simply resolve: *By the grace of God I devote my life wholly to the service of Christ's kingdom!* The external forsaking of home and going abroad is often a great help to the foreign volunteer, through the struggle it costs him and the breaking away from all that could hinder him. The home volunteer may have to continue in his calling, and not have the need of such an external separation, so he needs all the more the help which a pledge, secret or in union with others, can bring. The blessed Spirit can make it a crisis and a consecration that leads to a life utterly devoted to God.

Students in the school of obedience, study the last and great commandment well. Accept it with your whole heart and place yourselves entirely at His disposal.

3. Begin at Once To Act on Your Obedience

In whatever circumstances you are, it is your privilege to have within reach souls that can be won for God. And all around you there are numberless forms of Christian activity which invite your help and offer you theirs. Look upon yourself as redeemed by Christ for His service, as blessed with His Spirit to give you the very disposition that was in Him, and humbly but boldly take up your life calling of helping in the great work of winning back the world to God. Whether you are led of God to join some of the many agencies already at work or to walk in a more solitary path, remember not to regard the work as that of your church, or society, or as your own—but as the Lord's. Cherish carefully the consciousness of "doing it unto the Lord," of being a servant who is under orders, and simply carrying them out. Then your work will not come between you and your fellowship with Christ, as it does often, but it will link you inseparably to Him, His strength, and His approval.

It is easy to become so engrossed in the human interest there is in our work that its spiritual character, the supernatural power needed for it, the direct working of God in us and through us—all that can fill us with true heavenly joy and hope—is crowded out. Keep your King on His throne. Before He gave the command and pointed His servants to the great field of the world, He first drew their eyes to himself on the throne. "*All power is given me in heaven and on earth.*" It is the vision, the faith of Christ on the throne, that reminds us of the need and assures us of the sufficiency of His divine power. Obey, not a command, but the living Almighty Lord of Glory. Faith in Him will give you heavenly strength.

Those words preceded the command to make disciples. And then there followed, *"Lo, I am with you alway."* It is not only the glorious vision of Christ on the throne that we need, but Christ with us here below, in His abiding presence working for us and through us. Christ's power in heaven, Christ's presence on earth—between these two pillar promises lies the gate through which the Church enters for the conquest of the world. Let us follow our Leader, receive from Him our orders as to our share in the work, and never falter in the vow of obedience that has given itself to live wholly for His will and His work alone.

Such a beginning will be a training time, preparing us fully to know and follow His leading. If His pleading call for the millions of dying heathen comes to us, we shall be ready to go. If His providence does not permit our going, our devotion at home will be as complete and intense as if we had gone. Whether it be at home or abroad, if only the ranks of the obedient, the servants of obedience, the obedient unto death, are filled up, Christ shall have His heart's desire, and His glorious thought—the Gospel to every creature— shall find its accomplishment!

Blessed Son of God! Here I am. By Your grace, I give my life to the carrying out of Your last great command. Let my heart be as Your heart. Let my weakness be as Your strength. In Your name I take the vow of complete and lasting obedience. Amen.